Sayling the Babel

Sayling the Babel

poems and songs

Hylda Sims

Hearing Eye

Published by Hearing Eye 2006

Hearing Eye
Box 1, 99 Torriano Avenue
London NW5 2RX, UK
email: books@hearingeye.org
www.hearingeye.org

Poems © Hylda Sims 2006
Music and lyrics © Hylda Sims except the music to the song *Canvas of Dawn*,
which is taken from *Tzigani*, by Chris Haigh © 1998 JW Media Music Ltd.

ISBN: 1-905082-07-X

Acknowledgements
Some of these pieces have been published previously in these magazines: Orbis, Smith's Knoll,
Hallmark, Stand – and anthologies: *In the Company of Poets* (Hearing Eye), *Plant Care; A
Festschrift for Mimi Khalvati* (Linda Lee Books), *Parents* (Enitharmon), *London* (Enitharmon), *What
Poets Eat* (Foolscap), *Home* (Katabasis), *Making Worlds* (Headland).

I would like to thank the talented and helpful people who have made this collection possible:
John Rety, Susan Johns & Martin Parker for the book itself, Diz Disley for the chords to *Dark
Old Storm Cloud* and Simon Prager for rediscovering them. Chris Haigh for lending me his
beautiful fiddle tune, *Tzigani*. Special thanks to Tim Israel for his invaluable work transcribing
and in many instances arranging the music. Goldsmith's Poetry Workshop and The Poetry
School's excellent courses have been crucial in realising these poems. – H.S.

Poems are reasonably comfortable on a page, songs tend to feel imprisoned by paper.
These songs will shortly be freed onto CD. For details visit www.hylda.co.uk

This publication has been made possible with
the financial support of Arts Council England

Printed and bound by Cambridge University Press
Designed by Martin Parker at www.silbercow.co.uk

Cover: 'The City Ramblers' painting by Russell Quáy c1958

Contents

* *From* 'Reaching Peckham'

For Viv, Rom, Lily, Wilfe, Rufus & Remus

INTRODUCTION

Confessions of a Poetry Slave

Seven year spell on top of the buses through Dulwich and Walworth and
    over the Thames
and a walk through the Garden, from Strand to Long Acre by way of the Opera
and up Drury Lane
to my Saturday fiefdom, my heartbeat of London
a strange little street that's not quite in the frame
this poetry café not everyone goes to
but everyone there
knows my name

where we stake out the chairs and drag round the sofas and stack up the tables
and count out the float and set out the fliers and screw up the mic-stand
and plug in the cables and answer the questions and field the suggestions
and I try to be cool and urbane
but hold my breath hoping there's no football matches
no thunder and lightning, no jams on the streets and no strikes on the trains
no rival attractions where Heaney and Duffy
might sign their collections
and nobody's thought of
our name

The evening begins and I sit there just praying that no floor performer
will read a long lecture that goes on forever
or chant off by memory some just written effort
that's tedious and lame
and forget halfway through and go back to the start and then read it all
    over again
or some wild would-be rapper will rise to the challenge, all loud and insistent
and rude and discordant, all stamping and pointing and prancing and hamming
and frankly inane
and it won't do a thing
for our name

There's an artist we've booked who won't answer the emails, there's no
    information
I can't do the flier or send off to Time Out the plugs and the plaudits,
her grand reputation, the rumours put out that they'll make her a dame;
so only ten takers, no wonder I'm jumpy, the whole place is empty
not me who's to blame.
Oh the skill and the fire of this world renowned poet
folks surely must know it, folks surely would be here
folks would have been keen
if only they'd seen
her name

And then on the Monday a note from some floor spot who'd sadly been
    told not
to read for as long as the floor spot before'd got
(who'd sneaked in two poems pretending they're one)
and his art was demeaned and it seemed so unfair and why don't I explain
and I'm fed up with writing back notes to these losers to butter their egos
but his life is so bleak, he'll be upset all week
he might wait by the door, weeping out in the street
or he'll put the word round we're a bit of a clique and somehow we'll get
a bad name

Oh the times when the audience troop off up the stairs when the main
    reading's over
they say they must go for their transport to Dover
or Derby or Selby and isn't it lovely
being up there to share with the just-finished poet
this moment of love and acclaim
while amazing musicians who're swinging and groovy
are left in the cellar to play to themselves, it's a shame
and I feel like directing a stream of abuse at these philistine gits
who don't care what they miss
but I'm not a fascist and they paid all the same
so I stay down and listen and clap that much harder and plead for an encore

they play a request
in my name

Oh the nights when the clapped out PA starts to crackle
and the drinkers upstairs make a hell of a racket
and the coffee machine starts to rumble and whistle
as a solemn old poet of nation-wide fame
starts a soft-voiced recital of elegant verse to the hushed and respectful,
the plum-in-the-mouth and the great and the good (yes the buggers all came)
while I'm upstairs and down on these creaking old floorboards
trying to shut up the chatter and cut out the static, getting shocks for my trouble
and thinking, fuck this for a game
and this male prima donna
won't even remember
my name

It's well after midnight they're still sitting up there
talking Hooker and Hacker and getting much drunker
and God knows how long they'll remain,
the barperson's putting the chairs on the tables and snuffing the candles
and if black looks were cudgels they'd leave without brains
and I'm being quite polite, pleading, time you were leaving
and attempting to bundle them out in the rain
and at last they go staggering, carousing and swearing
and that means the neighbours complain
we're creating a nuisance we could lose our licence
and I know that we'll lose
our good name

And now here we are
it's the very last session
this show's going to move into memory lane
but I'd hate you to get a mistaken impression
I've not had a ball for I've loved every minute
the words and the music and getting to choose it

the organisation and every one in it
the improvisation and learning to do it
and being a link in the poetry chain

I've loved it for smallness and lightness and kindness
for talent and trust and the team mucking in
for the people who sang and the people who read
the people who played and the people who listened
to every inflection of what poets said.
I'm not being presumptuous or getting pretentious
but it's all seemed a little like guarding a flame
a flare of goodwill in the heart of the world
while the big movers out there are trying to douse it
producing bad movies and banning live music
and selling blockbusters for thousands of dollars
promoting crap telly for ill-gotten money
all out for celebrity power and gain
those business-school scholars, those cloth-eared white collars
are generally driving the future insane
and despite all the bitching I'm really just itching
to do it again and again and again
in my name

written for the last night of Poetry & Jazz at the Poetry Café,
Covent Garden. 19th March 2005

I Ain't Gauguin Blues   (may be sung to any twelve bar blues)

I'm sittin' on Tahiti drinkin' palm wine and coconut juice
Got the sea got the surf, drinkin' palm wine and coconut juice
Promotion to Papeete, an offer I could not refuse

Got this lonesome feelin', feelin' I can't seem to lose
Got this far off lonesome feelin', feelin' I just can't lose
Got this cravin' for Belgravia, got the take me back to London blues

Don't want these warm sea breezes, walkin' without any shoes
Don't like these balmy sea breezes, walkin' on the beach without my shoes
Got a yen for Big Ben, got the take me back to London blues

I want the grey sky up above me, disasters on the south-east news
I want the rain clouds gatherin', misery on the TV news
And I could kill for Piccadilly, got the take me back to London blues

I want to breathe in the pollution, stand in the rush hour queues
I want to freak out on the fumes, crush in the rush hour queues
Got a tube train brain, got the take me back to London blues

Don't like this lobster from the ocean and all this tax-free booze
Give me a burger and a Bud, not all this fresh seafood and tax-free booze
I'd try a Wagamama noodle, got the take me back to London blues

I'm stranded on Tahiti, drinkin' palm wine and coconut juice
Won't you fly me out of paradise and drop me back in SE22
Don't you know my name ain't Gauguin, got the take me back to London blues

My Guitar

doesn't exactly weep, she groans
a grumbly, clacky sort of sound
        kerrum bumbly choo chi bah wa

she'd like go on the road, hop
a freight car down to the Delta
ride the rod, tangle in the blue fingers
of Muddy Waters, bend a note or two
with B B or T-Bone, rest her heart
in the scarred hand of Jango
        kerrum bumbly choo chi bah wah

she's bored fretless with
this same old lick, longs for a trip
to the top of the neck, a progression
from the foothills of A flat
to the mountains of D sharp, a clutch
of lost chords, she can't take much more
of this folksy clawhammer picking
always in that missionary key of E
so long she's had to endure this same groove
        kerrum bumbly choo chi bah wah

My guitar is like a woman married all those years
to a man with only three positions
always putting his hat on the same chair
always hanging his grey overcoat on the same peg
always saying there's nothing else to be done
        kerrum bumbly choo chi bah wah

My guitar can't understand that I can't understand her
she murmurs a wild secret twang
learned from trees and spun metal
I don't have the tongue
there's no ears in my fingertips
I only play Pidgin
me longtime all thumb strummer
me few chord kerlacker lacker plunk thrasher
        kerrum bumbly choo chi bah wah

Oh, your versatile strings, your stretched, pearl-studded neck
your small-waisted, sonorous brown body
waiting like sleeping beauty to be kissed awake…
You don't deserve me, my guitar gently groans –
I've never taught her to weep

Your Old Guitar

Your Old Guitar

What's that gull I hear, crying to the sea
Seems to be a hound dog growling, howling to be free
Listen to the rainstorm drumming with a deep and heavy beat
Nothing but your old guitar walking down the street

What's that sound I see where the sun breaks through
Sliding down a rainbow's back, fifty colours blue
I can hear the four winds humming, dreaming up a tune
Nothing but your old guitar reaching for the moon

    Chinese firecrackers on a coal black sky
    Symphony of last year's summer and the night train rattling by
    Mail man calling, early in the morning
    Hoochy coochy rhythm of the day returning
    Cool, cool, as the polar star
    Just your old guitar

What's that stream out there, talking to a tree
In the moochy smoochy shade where deserts used to be
I can hear a wild world thrumming, in a long lost key
Nothing but your old guitar making love to me

The Bassplayer and the Bandleader's Wife

You played the bass, you were just seventeen
and talented; your hair, your eyelashes
were pale and long, they swept me off my feet
and turned my legs to quavers. We were rash
as well as wrong, but it was such a passion
we had no sense to spare. You spread your coat
on stony ground behind the Ritzy: the splash
of rain, lights from the street, we seem to float
as if that old bomb site were sea, and we were boat

and in our slipstream what'd been solid ground
was maelstrom, nothing that was built could stand
my life was lost, my loved ones nearly drowned.
We two were washed on separate spits of land
in separate oceans – you joined a touring band
whilst I, clutching to wrack and flotsam, tried
to find my way back home; on every hand
were shipwrecks; lamps along the street beside
the flea-pit burned cold and yellow, this was winter tide…

We meet by chance, you're fifty something, you've grown
wide open. *It took me years*, you say, *I loved you
so much*. This guilt I've carried on my own
for ages, lifts, becomes a ballad, two
voices reprising a song. We wear our new
faces, settled and plain; this secret scar
identifies us still, a rendezvous
deep in the shell, where all the best pearls are,
All posh, the Ritzy now…   I know, three screens, a bar

Skiffle Days   (Frankfurt 1956 – for Chris Bateson)

Everyone is eating cakes
every cake has cream
round every table solid *Damen* wearing fruit tart hats
put away great hills of cream
deftly moving two-pronged silver forks
so we scarcely see the ferrying
of pastry stacks, Camelot towers of choux
minarets of marzipan, battlements of Battenburg
decorated, overlaced, lightly spliced with cream,
to briefly parted mouths, as they chat
unmoglich! ...sie sind so... und... so...
staring upon us unabashed
the way we English can't

Grimy from kipping in the van
we have our busking money stacked and counted
tidy piles of pfennigs, a mark note or two
the tip's been calculated in

Chris has ordered *apfeltorte*
mit doppel sahne. He would.
Does he have cream! The pastry buckles
disappears beneath this snowdrift mosque
this cloud, this cumulus
of cream

Were his fingers busy with his ears
pressing the trumpet stops, listening
to Louis in his head, pedalling a high sweet C
when the slender tuning fork
slipped from underneath,

allowed his cloud, his gloat, his Bunter's dream
of cream to slide, to float, to glide
to plop, to splatter
on his dirty jeans, his ragged pumps
this spotless German floor?

And does he steal the show as ever
holding up a foaming paw, murmuring,
quite calmly, (no translation needed)
I seem to have this cream...

And don't these Frankfurt burgeresses
clap and shriek and laugh
and buy us all another round of cakes

What a Miracle

A Russian quintet busking outside Dorothy Perkins
in Ipswich, popular classics, Bizet, Gounod and good
two silver cornets, tuba, tarnished trombone and curly French horn
all their notes perfect and clean, working
so well together you don't uncover the horn till you've stood
a little to pick out its shy middle tones, like the dawn

lingering and strolling under the day-breaking trumpets
over the night-hearted tuba completing the chord
Welcome from St Petersburg students, a notice says
propped on a trombone case, *Ochen Xorosho*, I murmur, crumpling
a fiver which I wonder if I can afford
then remember who I am and throw it in the case

remember how I've always been a busker's moll
how my first lover played the violin in an arcade
below Trafalgar Square, the Bach Busker, he was a red
and Jewish and could never play at all
for a captive audience, there because they'd paid
he only felt safe when they were led

by the ear to his unexpected delicate vibrato
behind the thrum of buses and cars,
able to stroll past or just stand there
listening to the fierce bowed chords and spiccato
deflecting from shop windows and the milk bar
on the corner into perfectly composed air.

I stand now, listening to the band
tearful, while the citizens of Ipswich
gather and pass, gather and pass... where these five lads,
whose grandparents never saw London and Amsterdam
or Ipswich and loved Joseph Stalin and Vladimir Illych
Lenin, because things got fairer than they had

been, are now playing, *When I'm Sixty-Four*
maybe for me (I've been here some time) a deep oom pah pah
from the tuba, the trumpets sounding transatlantic
now, French horn quoting the counter-melody with a flare
trombone bending in some Gershwinny wah wah,
notes golden as a Kremlin dome but democratic

Kakaya chuda! As my Russian teacher said
the day she heard they'd put a man in space

kakaya chuda – what a miracle   *Ochen Xhorosho* – very good

Jamming

You fingered a Gibson guitar
by a pond, shucked off your high-heeled
sneakers, dunked your feet
through floating leaves. Cool.
I fell in love with you that day
some daytime gig, Ringmer, wasn't it?

> He played the bass in four four time
> New Orleans marching beat
> He slapped that bass in four four time
> A real New Orleans beat
> He made her feel the Rose and Crown
> Was down on Bourbon Street

Another day trip, Brighton is it?
this couple paddling near the edge
he lobster-shelled, trousers rolled
her undressed knees veined marble
an FM breeze kisses their heads
Christ, he shouts, have they got cloth ears!

> He's lived in twelve bars all his life
> Oh Lord that's all he's got
> Hung round in twelve bars all his life
> Good lord that's all he's got
> She'd like some wild new funky man
> Still slim, still sweet, still hot

Chords augment, diminish, suspend
syncopate to sea, beyond the rock
waves crash in like snare drums,
Every damn thing's amplified these days
musical cripples with synthesizers,
Daddy, we started it, she thinks

She can't recall those fine blonde curls
Those moochy, smoochy eyes
She can't recall that fine brown frame
Those hoochy coochy thighs
All Muddy Waters through the toes
His come on, *Baby, baby*
Baby, baby, baby
Oh baby, can you sing the blues?

Canvas of Dawn

Dawn walks on the roof, paints the first leaf, opens your eyes
Your waking hands touching my face, conjuring space out of the night
    Love, I feel your mouth on my mouth
    Birds of the morning starting to fly south
    See how the sky measures the room
    Sculptures each form on the canvas of dawn

Dawn carves every bush, sketches a rose, stipples the sea and makes
    your lips
Remember the sun, the way rivers run to be salty and free
    Love, I feel the curve of your skin
    Daylight unfolds you, shades your colours in
    Your sleepy smile, your sheltering arms
    Naked and warm on the canvas of dawn

Cliff Hangers

In the pub, old boys, moved in from the south
perch, grey parrots, boasting, roosting,
opposite, the smoke hoose (as they say up here)
unwinds a scarf of kipper-scented grey
into a black, travelling sky

We walk along the coastal path, past
bungalows, allotments, soon fields of cows
slope to a cliff, sheer, curving round a shore
of black whinstone and scoops of beach.
Across the face hundreds of birds

kittiwakes, sit breast on breast
cuddled on rock ledges, their guano,
marking time, thickened to white lace,
audience to the lift and lull of tides
curtainfalls of cloud

April snow flurries the high hedges
of whitethorn, merges with blossom, melts
in our plastic cups of tea, falls
on our sandwiches, forms crystals
on his red hair then blows over

He scrambles through a patch of heather
finds a spur of whin where breakers turn
whirlpooling spouts of foam on him
in his navy scarf and anorak
he watches the kittiwakes fish

and I watch him – he capers near the edge
leans over, flaps his wings, pretends
to be a gull, a jagged cross beneath
the old smooth wheel of birds, inapt as Cnut
before the riff and buff of waves

Kittiwakes, wide-armed, screaming, drop
in the sea's open throat, held on a feather
I climb over, pull him back, back to the pub
where there are parrot stories, smoke and kippers
people playing darts

Baltimore

♩=86

D   G   D

You came in borr - ow- ing the west wind_

6 G   D

Foll - ow- ing the curr -ents and the breeze_____ Your

10   G   D

hair was tang -led and your eyes skimmed____

14 G

A -cross that spang-led sum -mer sea_____ And I

18 A⁷   D

fell in love   with   you sail - a - way For the

22 A⁷   D

songs you sang____ and the chords you could play For your

26 C   D

trans - at - lan - tic   talk_____   and the

29 C   D

eas - y clothes you   wore_____   And you

Baltimore

You came in borrowing the west wind
Following the currents and the breeze
Your hair was tangled and your eyes skimmed
Across that spangled summer sea
And I fell in love with you Sailaway
For the songs you sang and the chords you could play
For your transatlantic talk & the easy clothes you wore
You told me you'd sailed all the way from Baltimore

I pointed out the way to Casablanca
You joked, 'Here's lookin' at you twice'
Along the beach your sailboat rode at anchor
You said, 'This sure is paradise'
And I took you home, that very same day
To my one-room house on the far side of the bay
And we lived four seasons through by the ocean's open door
Where the transatlantic tankers ride to Baltimore
    You silenced time with your fingertips
    A certain smile played around your lips
    Sometimes I'd see you frown as the westbound ships passed by
    And the salt from the spray left a tear, one small tear, in your eye

This love would never last a lifetime
I guess we knew that from the start
This love was langoustines and white wine
A little tapas for the heart
Just a pair of gulls in an empty sky
With no angry words and no asking why
With no clouds ahead and no life before
Till a message in a bottle came from Baltimore

Your voice a song that I can't quite hear
Your twisted smile seems to disappear
The memory of you thins and stretches into space
And the tide pulls out leaving sand in its place

You came in borrowing the west wind
Following the currents of your mind
You must have known that you were destined
To leave my grieving heart behind
When I fell in love with you Sailaway
I never guessed your name till the very last day
I should have known you'd go back to that transatlantic shore
And a girl waiting there for you in Baltimore

Digestif

The love café offered everything free
bread was served on a high bed of cushions
salt too,

a melange of exotic fruits – wild apples
plantain, fig, sun-stroked on Persian rugs in
hot June

The menu promised winter meats
spiced, marinaded; fair-bodied wines
dew scented

and for dessert, flaring on night's skillet
spiked with rue, saucy as dreams
la lune flambée

A new customer, shady, hungry, thin
saw the signs, came in, tasted for flavour
poached the chef

Our fond café served bread and salt...
mangoes. I remember,   the stone
still in my gut

Constantly Connected

He phoned at 0.100 hours
from a call box in Casablanca, cut
he told me he loved me
till nuclear waste turns garden mulch
and rain forests rise up in Wapping

rang at 0.200 hours
from Moosehead, Maine, merry
to tell me he loved me
till the M1 runs beneath the plough
and trains again to Adlestrop

gave me a buzz at 0.300 hours
from Vishnarva, Estonia, wrecked on vodka
told me he loved me
till 4-wheel drives turn into bikes
and microchips crumble to moondust

giving me a tinkle around dawn
from Leatherhead, Surrey, reversing the charges
he told me he loved me
till libraries open all night long
and Sainsbury's close on Sundays

I told him *I* loved *him*
till the neighbour's stereo plays Bach
till car alarms refuse to shrill, but
I needed sleep, this miffed
his manly pride, the line went dead.

The nights are long and dark
as optic cables under the ocean
my love will telephone
when the lark sings on Canary Wharf
and William Blake in Westminster

Breakfast with my Demon Lover

Last night's pot-au-feu, dead candles
fag papers, ashtrays, melting butter
two glasses purpled at the bottom
core of pippin, five days old
rind of brie —
plateau of left things, best seen by night

Blackened saucepan, lacking handle
lidless teapot, blunted knives
creaking door that won't stay shut
wine-stained lino, row of bottles
green and growing
the morning is unnaturally bright

Cracked vase, ten roses dangle
(all these foolish things gone metric)
pouting their wilting crimson lips
leafless buds with broken necks —
Old Nick's gift
Make some coffee, he's groaning, *pass me a light*

Eyes bedforsaken, hair in tangles,
stubbled chin, distinctly cleft,
propped on a hairy, nail-chewed paw
blue vapour curls up from his nostrils
dragon's breath
Bit of a mess, he gloats, I say, *Yeah, quite!*

He's made the place his own, a vandal
satisfied, taking his ease
this smoking head, bum on one chair
feet propped up against another
devil's prick
king of underwork and oversight

Know what, you're a fucking scandal,
I say, he drains his cup and yawns,
stretches, *Time for a man to split,*
the sky turns dark, thunder crashes
a lightning flash
hoofprints on the stairs. Whiff of cordite

These foolish things

Dead candles
faint hang of joss
two glasses, purpled at the bottom
staining the flat white graves
of murdered poems

these foolish things my love
remind me of you

and five red roses
no thorn nor leaf
pouting their darkly folded lips
petals infused with blood
from secret tongues

a hand of roses
one for my mouth
one for my ear
two for my eyes
one to lay upon my coffin

these foolish thoughts my love
remind me of you

and lit candles
scent of cypress
empty chalice
a mind
white as unborn lines

Measuring Up

The thing we're shifting doesn't fit
in the space that waits for it
it won't go through the door
or round the corners
checking beforehand ought to warn us
but it isn't out by more
than an eighth of an inch
I always think that, at a pinch

things'll squeeze in.
It's an original sin
to believe that deal and chipboard
are similar to wool,
malleable
they're not, and I've ignored
your words, you've got all the weight
we're struggling, trying to keep it straight

Now there's a spare chest of drawers
on the landing, stranded, mine of course.
We lie there back to back
most of the night
you sulking, me contrite
leaving a draughty crack
not quite an eighth of an inch,
we touch and part, trying to flinch

Strangers

Strangers

Don't count on me, I'm just a loser
And I can't be your guiding star
Never could refuse your love or choose it
I'm a stranger here, as you are
For every question there's ten answers
And then a hundred questions more
Fortune never smiles, she merely glances
You're not the only one she's looking for
    We're lost, without a rhyme or a reason
    Leaves shaken off a tree
    Lost, it's the human condition
    What you get is what you see
    Don't go blaming me
    When you're lost you're free

Sat down with a shrink in Tobermory
Listened to a preacher on Capri
Dressed in different clothes, the same old story
Don't think too much, just follow me
For every fact, there's twenty fictions
For every truth, a hundred lies
And if you spot the contradictions
You're not welcome in their paradise
    We're lost, without a song or a season
    Stones rolling down the scree
    Lost, it's a slippery position
    We might not be home for tea
    Don't go blaming me
    When you're lost you're free

Don't count on me, I'm just a minstrel
And I can't read the notes you write
Nothing can be sung, unless it sings well
Here is no scented rose, no pale moonlight
For every chord there's ten inversions
For every tune, it's counterpart
With every take, the soundtrack worsens

There are no verses left to learn by heart
    We're lost without a might or a maybe
    Off the piste without a ski
    Lost and it's *Who loves you baby?*
    Not a soul that I can see
    Don't go blaming me
    When you're lost you're free

Bumped into a broker in Milwaukee
Heard a politician make a speech
Everything they said conspired to bore me
Those weasel words of diplomacy
For every deal a devastation
For every prince ten million poor
And if you rise above your station
You won't remember where you lived before
    We're lost without a fund or a fashion
    In Berkeley Square without a key
    Lost, not a pavement to crash on
    In the throes of bankruptcy
    Don't go blaming me
    When you're lost you're free

Don't count on me, I'm just a loner
And I can't be your helping hand
Everything you touch, you want to own it
There's nothing left my friend, no promised land
For every god there's fifty faces
For every faith a hundred more
Half a billion stars just died in space as
We turned the lights down low and closed the door
    We're lost without a moon or a mission
    A beach ball floating out to sea
    Lost on a doomed expedition
    It's the only place to be
    Ride the waves with me
    Ah can't you see
    We're lost, we're lost, we're lost – we're free

Here's Lookin' at You, Kid

In Praise of Younger Men

His jeans don't have to support
his belly, the hems
rest on hunky DMs

He has left his father's closet
where sad suits hung like shrouds
in camphor clouds

He'll pose, artless as a butterfly
round his svelte body he'll throw
my kimono

He conjures intimate soul feasts
from peppers, pulses and stock
magicked in a wok

He will light scented candles to me
make love in their sensuous glow
does he know

I adore looking at him?
I only wish he
would stop looking at me

Here's to You, Mrs Robinson

In Praise of Older Women

The gift of heart, intelligence, a chance
of eloquence

came through her fingertips, creating fusion
set his fashion

of thoughts, his history unpenned and slim
till she read him

her keystrokes editing, she turns his unborn
pages, he learns

his character by touch, paragraphs
of unformed, rough

fancies she fingers to shape, creating stories
philosophies

Where he was muscle and skin, nape and navel
he becomes novel

Requitement

It's lots of little things, too small
to mention, make me see I can't
love you; it isn't looks, you aren't
unkind or stupid, not at all

It's when you constantly say, *Real time*
that sort of mopped-up psycho-phrase
Denial, you'd say, my distaste,
that intolerance of mine

But words evolve us, every choice
leads to a different branch, a break
a species turn, a path we take
the only map we have is voice

Real time implies an unreal one,
I'd say, but then you'd simplify
at length on worlds I don't deny
exist, but won't consign to jargon

Our forbears fell from different trees
that is the crux – you tiptoe when
you go barefoot, now and again
I see you run like that: these

are spores of ancestry, your line
was cloven-hooved I'm sure, gnu
or zebra, moose or caribou
whilst mine was quilled, like porcupine

close to the earth, the night time shift
spines a-scribble and a-rattle
while you, nomadic plains cattle,
followed the wind and the herd's drift

It's in our genes, ancient as chalk
we're animals that can't discover
how to mate, or eat each other –
and please don't say, *We need to talk...*

and now you ask the question, *Do you
love me?* A pause. The air goes dense.
Well, actually... I feel a sense
of failure, cowardice ...*I do.*

You smile your wide, believing smile,
another irritation, why
do you believe me when I lie?
Now you seem happy for a while

like a child's balloon, you rise
I'd like to prick you with a pin
but couldn't bear to see you, thin
with grief, and madness in your eyes

again. I know that we aren't fit
together, trapped and insincere
I stroke your horns and draw you near
because I love you, dear, a bit

Xanadu

Xanadu

Summer's a dancer, always on the move
Autumn days are few
Winter comes, as come she must
Spring's a blade of dew
    Seed, leaf and snow
    A year full of days gone
    Turn and turn and fall
    You are my still and perpetual season
    Holding them all

Night's a chancer, never shows his hand
Till his game is through
Moon can argue black is white
Dawn's a point of view
    Noon runs to dusk
    A day full of hours gone
    Turn and turn of the tide
    You are my sunrise, my chorus of birdsong
    Broad daylight

Life's a stranger, on a northbound train
Can't tell where it's travelling to
Time's a track that won't run back
Love is Xanadu
    Hill, field and plain
    A road full of miles gone
    Turn and turn of the wheel
    You are my steppe, my mysterious horseman
    Riding to the sea

To Winifred

It's my birthday, I'm alone
like the night I came naked
from the sea, birthdays
are bringing me towards you

One look, you fell in love
immediately, cord
around my neck, all ready,
naked, from your sea

You kept me at your breast
constantly, carried me
everywhere, sang to me
your eyes
followed my eyes
jealous of every flicker
when you fed me, you

were fulfilled
when I spoke you laughed
imitated me
and cooed, I longed
to tell you everything

But your constant attention
to my detail proved
too much to parry
now I longed
to be where nobody
could admire my likeness
see the open pride

with which I was exhibited, as if
you'd painted me yourself, which
of course
you had

I kept my words
under my breath, fearful
you would steal my thoughts and I
would ruin yours

I'm alone, naked
on my birthday
in the tower you built for me
your great-grandchildren
have swum in
from the sea

You wouldn't believe
how strong I've grown
since you departed
how nothing that you gave to me
was wasted
after all
how carefully
I've made this card:
thankyou for
the birthday, with love
to you, from me

Left Rites

When mum, who never quit the Party,
died, the Red Army turned up.
Her Co-op Bentley, English as boot black
trailing limos, slowed through Norwood Cemetery
where Mrs Beeton's bones are stocked
and gothic piety has run to fruit

They stood, peaks, epaulettes, a host
of scarlet stars, flanked by cherubs
epitaphs, cracked angels. Rolling down
the limo glass, I winked, a Cossack,
shamefaced, flushing, dived
behind the BBC pantechnicon

By the chapel, Zils purred, inside, a comrade
spoke her casket slid, her anthem rang
and the last fight… The verger, not one of us
switched off our tape too soon before
the Internationale unites
the human race, but sure as the sky

dawns rosy over Dulwich, she watched – lights,
rolling, take thirteen – the Beeb shoot *Stalin*
and chortled home with us to bourgeois tea
where, tossing down vodka, clenching our fists
we drank to Trotsky, Lenin, Marx, mother's jokes

Putting Pennies on the Line

Those days we'd get up in the dark, goosepimpling
crumpling socks and hankies in our cases
scrambling for breakfast as the black Welsh morning

thins to grey, night lingering on our faces;
sun, cutting towards Moelwyn and Moelwyn Bach
slices mountains off the sky, lost spaces

wake into trees and cliffs below Moelwyn Fach;
us, climbing the slatey hill by the mystery
of village, past the Pengwern Hotel, up the path

into Llan station, under the canopy, blistery
with brown paint. Benny and Don are down the end
by the crossing; the stationmaster, paunched and whiskery,

stumps, suspicious, the train cranks round the bend,
the two boys slyly scuttle down, spring back,
the train stops, breathes out, they crouch forward again

Iesy Gris, the guard swears, *get off the track*!
We pull them in, laughing and tumbling
the seven oval pennies warm and cracked

under the rocks to Blaenau the train clatters and hoots
valleys stretching out to dry all along the pylons
slate miners off to work, taste of steam and soot
riding down to London, doodlebug and siren

The Ballad of William James

♩=112

Em   **A⁷**   **D**

Will - iam James was sent to pub - lic school

3   **Em**   **A⁷**   **D**

Had to stand in line for as - sem - bly in the morn - ing A

5   **Em**   **A⁷**   **D**

sur - ly sea of grey full of fidg - et - ing and yawn - ing

7   **Em**   **A⁷**   **D**   rall.

Buzz - ing through his brain went the tell-ing off and warn-ing While

9   **G**   **Em⁷**   **A**   **D**   **F♯⁷**   **Bm**   **Em**

some - where in the sun we kids were hav-ing fun at Sum-mer

11   **A**   **D**   **Em⁷**   **A⁷**

hill_____ At Sum - mer - hill_____ at Sum - mer-

13   **Bm**   **Em⁷**   **A**

hill

58

The Ballad of William James

William James was sent to public school
Had to stand in line for assembly in the morning
A surly sea of grey full of fidgeting and yawning
Buzzing through his brain went the telling-off and warning
While somewhere in the sun we kids were having fun at Summerhill

William James would dream of girls in class
Passed a silly note with F words as a feature
When he got found out, said *It wasn't only me, Sir*
Got beaten by his chums and a caning from his teacher
It's not against the rule to swim naked in the pool at Summerhill

William James could never tell a soul
Couldn't tell his Pa, he'd be sure to get another
Had to be a man, not go blubbing to his mother
Hid it in his head, like a corpse inside a cupboard
It isn't a disgrace when tears run down your face, at Summerhill

William James goes back to school today
Had a troubled night with dreams of blood and thunder
Had to take a pill to keep his breakfast under
Screwed his mouth up tight so he wouldn't make a blunder
The first kids to arrive run shouting down the drive at Summerhill

William James grew up to be a judge
Underneath his wig, a pile of bones lay hidden
Screwed his mouth up tight as he sent boys off to prison
Got an OBE as a man of strength and vision
But every child of mine gets love sent down the line from Summerhill

Seascape with Train

The tide is going out
on salt pastures sand has covered,
the train a long brush-stroke removing itself.

He sits opposite another passenger
a woman unwrapping sandwiches
a faint flexing of lips reveals
her English taste for lonely journeys

his thumbs fondle each other, retreat
inside the cave of his palms
he gazes out of the window, grey eyes
reflecting exteriors:

what a coast! Absolutely flat,
stick-limbed birds picking about
could you understand why they strut
float on waves, suddenly fly…

and the train, obvious old metaphor
shunting, rattling to the terminus,
had we not invented it ourselves
wouldn't God construct it for us?

She's finishing her sandwiches
putting the wrapper, scraps of crust
tidily in her bag, brushing at crumbs
if you could fathom a woman's thoughts…

he needs to float words, find currents...
So strange, the birds, he rasps. She smiles
brows knotting, but polite, *Birds? Ah, yes, the birds...*
aren't they... It tells him nothing.

Both of them stare out – the sand is wet
shines a moment as the sea recedes
perhaps the tide is turning
beginning to come in.

The train sings to itself, seems
suspended in empty land running back;
underneath, time gossips, chatters
across the points

Sayling the Babel

(Drinté Mog 1499)

We sommé foglant an the starfoot
clammt und sveltstrickt
ins gnocchi nicht

Stilldeckt, fearboden
velblakket all
nem wan kans nils persicht

Oren bin oren drammet we
slepfe nem wan kannot
pensammé oft we nilgen usland sicht

Wendon, Lodblinken! Sonné rimmet
felts ab clair
bov blaugen sofar okean

Bretplumers flaum am doppled woterscuffs
skimflighters brostle, ayn gint notheran
strangé flishen, como gigants, glimt and plaumet

Sen kepitin Fortuno
(Lodreft bogfutch!)
smileeven

Fargript, mundklept, lagenflotted
we sommé gamboltongues
befor the wander of itt

Sailors on an early voyage of discovery to the new world speaking a European patois

I'm coasting into Peckham

lowlights reflecting
on my graphite wings

at the hospital
ambulances flashing
a bleeping on the wind

above the Sally Army building
obelisks prod me
towards heaven

I bank over the station
tiny drinkers by the Phoenix
toy trains rattling

follow the railway down
sketch in the nick, the pickle factory
(a whiff of onion)

Rye Lane is a red necklace
of buses, pavements beaded
with bargain shoppers

stalls down Choumert Road send up
a flare of foreign fruits
turbulence of reggae rocks me

concrete dominoes stack
little terraces fold away
behind me

the Rye, a grassy tablecloth,
sets out its vegan banquet
warm air holds me, I glide

a flock of geese,
a crimson kite
join me in the sky

Down Choumert Road

there's daffs, a quid three bunches
new season's spuds, thirty pence a pound
six limes fifty pence, fresh crimson chillies
capers, cardamoms, cumin, puzzles of ginger
eddoes, mangoes, melons, ackee, chow chow
pale dimpled breadfruit, manioc rough as bark

fans of skate on marble, shark fin, turbot
huss, bass, goat-fish, ink-fish in a bucket,
Goes well with custard, want some parsley with it ?
His rubbers slub a nifty riff, *Here George,*
he scuds a mullet; rhythm's pummelling on
from Blue Beat City – Rap and Ragga, Reggae
Hip-Hop, Ska; *Not like the old days*
is it, Mrs Lady? He winks, you won't remember,
cabbage, cod on Friday, forever Crosby
crooning Easter Bonnet on the wireless

Birdwatching

Each day they come, some black,
some speckled, brief statues
above the terracotta stack
mounted on the lip

Even on calm days it must
be cold this season; wind
up here, not fussed with leaves, gusts
unhindered, playing the sky

What's to be viewed? Some roofs,
our bald and wormless gardens,
a spire or two, thin smoke, the proofs
of alien habitation

What do they think of it?
Do their eyes align
things into colours, patterns fit
for birdsong, nesting country?

Telescopic vision's
just a phrase, no clue
to how a bird sitting on
a chimney feels, seeing

Top Floor

This morning there are three men on the roof
next door, chimney pointers. I expected
to be alone, with no external proof
that I exist, to potter, undetected
a nobody, a mouse, unheard, unseen
undressed, unwashed, the luxury of seclusion;
but we're a two-way television screen
a face-to-face, a parallel occasion:
them, edging round the tower of bricks
like tightrope men, in muddy bobble hats
and donkey jackets, pausing now to mix
new mortar, light up, hands around the match
and me here, sneaking coffee, timid guest
in someone else's airspace, dispossessed

On Not Writing My Novel

I get up, puzzle on a little poem
I eat a bowl of yoghurt, wash my clothes
then fetch the post and make the bed, too late
by now, I think, for getting down to prose
which can't be dreamed up in the bath; deadlines
is what I need – exactly what I've got:
dead lines, espaliered, rootless, black on white
to rearrange in miles of well-turned plot
all bedded in and diligently pruned
with every branchlet tensioned on a string;
meanwhile the sturdy poem grows and blooms,
self-watering, an independent thing
not much to do but turn it to the sun,
its stems will straighten up, its petals sing

Incident in Tooting

A misted sun, weekday morning, nothing
hints of deeds of violence before
the day is out. Curtains stir in Tooting
at number 5 a woman locks her door

she leaves, missing the postman with his wares
junk mail, letters, bills, receipts, a card
from Rome, a short plane ride, distant as Mars
At Tooting Bec the station walls are scarred

not la dolce vita this, not quite.
Pretty in a way, but pale and thin
her mouth so lip-gloss red, so office-neat –
the man who grabs the strap has just squeezed in

panting a bit, he bites his nail and stares
he rocks and rides, his eyes searching for hers

he rocks and rides, his eyes searching for hers
not old, not young with tousled hair, no tie
he hangs there, doesn't find a seat, prefers
to flex his legs, a speedy-exit guy

she thinks, putting him in a box, she's seen
his type before, all talk and somewhat cruel
her intuition, face not so much mean
as dark and haunted. God, she thinks, you fool

why speculate? You don't so much as know
this bloke, strap hanger, stranger, always late
always the last one on, his manner so
inscrutable, you wouldn't hesitate

to call him sinister: those eyes... some flaw
hints of deeds of violence, before...

Hints of deeds of violence before
had never surfaced in his mind, and yet
a certain predilection he now saw
had grown in him, a kind of appetite.

He'd watch her leave the house, then ring her bell
no one would be home, somehow, he thought
you knew she lived alone, you could just tell:
the name, the tidy front, the paperweight

inside the window, primly on the sill
a gift he guessed, or bought in Benidorm
a globe, an insect trapped in glass, and still
for company's sake a light left on; he'd run

the cars would prowl on by, some joker hooting
the day is out. Curtains stir in Tooting

The day is out, curtains stir in Tooting
across the Common pigeons start and scatter
schoolkids at the bus stop, wild and shouting
two neighbours by a fence, the usual natter

he'd stood behind a wall and scuffed his shoes
a milk cart passed, not often you see those
the sky declared its sex in pinks and blues
in these suburban streets a stranger shows

intruder, this is what he felt, and was
should he have worn a suit, or combed his hair?
If he had not, it must have been because
he'd had no fixed belief he'd end up there

again, and yet again, and then once more
at number 5 a woman locked her door…

At number 5 a woman locked her door
In the shower she'd pictured Tom, his skin
all bronzed and fit, his eyes a little more
romantic and sincere, his dimpled chin

the mail still hadn't come, she'd grabbed some breakfast
imagining the square, the trattorias
shady courtyards, olive trees and cypress
she'd thought him casual when he'd come to see her

to say goodbye. She wished he'd write, or call
she gulped more coffee, shrugged a jacket on
and left the centre light on in the hall
outside, the trees looked dusty in the sun

suburban solitude is hard to bear
she leaves, missing the postman with his wares

She leaves, missing the postman with his wares
elastic bands fall on the step, he shoves
the items through, they plummet down, sleep there
beside the mat as innocent as doves

that coo and chatter in the evening, later
after the office and the office dinner
where Ormalroyd in sales upsets the waiter
and Jones in stores remarks she's getting thinner

she'd made excuses, caught the tube, she'd had
three G and T's and two tequilas, and
the wine, but only felt confused and sad
couldn't face the gossip or the band.

The light inside the hall is yellow, hard
junk mail, letters, bills, receipts, a card

Junk mail, letters, bills, receipts ...a card
she stumbles on them, pushing through the door
a picture of the Coliseum, word
he's coming back at once, the reason – her

Just couldn't live without you. Life's so weird
the very day that other, who... *We meet
again*, he'd said, as if, before, they'd shared
a meal, a conversation or a sheet

not just the morning train, three times, with dozens
more. He'd leaned above her, everything
about him was mysterious but brazen...
she reads the card again, then hears the ring

That's him, she thinks, and runs back down the stairs,
from Rome – a short plane ride, distant as Mars

From Rome, a short plane ride, distant as Mars
now, Tom thought, waiting about beside
the carousel. And from the airport bar
he called, but no reply, he can't decide

what next, it's late, she should be back. He gets
the tube to Tooting Bec and rings her bell
but no reply, he rings again and waits...
is something missing from the windowsill?

Of course she still lives here, just get a grip,
he tells himself, she must be up in town
she's gone straight on from work, some office trip
she'll catch the last train back. He starts back down

the road. His suitcase makes the walking hard
at Tooting Bec the station walls are scarred

at Tooting Bec the station walls are scarred
with alien names in spray paint, red as blood
no one on the forecourt but a guard
pulling the gates across, but someone stood

beside a lamp post waiting silently
to catch a bus that's never going to come.
Beyond the shuttered shops Tom can just see
a sign for Toobec Mini Cabs, how numb

his fingers feel around the suitcase handle
the man beside the lamp post watches him
a beggar settles down beside his bundle
the station lights go flickering and dim

Tom changes arms and sets off down the street
not la dolce vita this, not quite…

Not la dolce vita this, not quite
he watches: beggar in a bag, some twit
suitcase in hand, who's missed his train, the night
plays on, twit gets a cab, the seconds slip

He's become detached, it doesn't frighten
him to stand here watching night spit out
these sad and meagre facts, his fingers tighten
round the globe as if they were a sort

of purchase on the world, some other world
he used to live in. He recalled it then
he'd met someone for lunch today, a girl
been watching her for days, he'd caught her train

and then caught her. It made his memory spin
pretty in a way, pale and thin

pretty in a way, pale and thin
but why he'd fixed on her, he didn't know
her legs, her walk, that teetering on the pin
-sized heels? The way she seemed alone? Below

him sitting on the train, she seemed to shrink
in size, he'd felt so dominant, so good
so brave, he didn't even stop to think
just blurted out his words: *Perhaps we could*

meet up for lunch today, been watching you
all week… she'd looked up slowly, she was cool
but flattered he could tell. He frowned but knew
he'd won. *I don't do pick-ups as a rule*

she'd said, and smiled. He'd craved to kiss her feet
her mouth, so lip-gloss red, so office-neat…

Her mouth so lip-gloss red, so office-neat
she stands beneath a tree in Regent's Park.
Tom took it on that day they'd gone to meet
her mother. Later in his dusty flat

they'd made a kind of promise to each other
not that they'd been absolutely sure
not then, except they'd spent six months together
and being the well-matched couple that they were

it seemed the thing to do. He'd no idea
that being away from her would be so tough
he'd kept the picture with him everywhere
afraid he lose her face, her smile, her laugh

he'd tried to sense her skin against his skin…
The man who'd grabbed the strap had just squeezed in

The man who'd grabbed the strap had just squeezed in
and taken her. She felt she understood
at once what kind of man he was. That grin
was calculating, cocksure and she should

have told him, no, but something in his eyes
had caused a kind of meltdown. Holding her breath
she'd slowed the moment further, met his gaze
and knowing this was danger, breathed out, *Yes*.

They'd met in the *Amalfi*, up in town
they ate and talked. She'd thought, it's two extremes
this stranger you've just met, but always known
somehow, but too intense, such crazy dreams

I have to go, she slips out through the doors…
panting a bit, he bites his nail and stares

Panting a bit he bites his nail and stares
around him, pays and leaves and walks the streets
till night puts on its flashy clothes and wears
its couples like a taunt. You're on your knees

because she's got away. How many times
have you done this before – a simple answer
never! You've stalked her, hid behind the limes
in some dull street in Tooting, just to glance her

going off to work and now you've let her
slip the hook. You've left yourself alone
and being alone is death, you know that better
than any monk. He takes the Northern Line

going south. Handsome is as handsome dares
he rocks and rides his eyes searching for hers…

Tom rocks and rides, his eyes searching for hers
six times he'd rung her bell, nine times her phone
he'd tried her work, was told she wasn't there
her mother didn't know where she had gone

he rides for days like that, he likes to hope
she'll step on board and smile and take her seat
She won't. The days'll pass. He'll learn to cope
sleep in the daytime, never clean his flat…

Those fingers tightened round the globe of glass
(heavy it was and slurred with blood) and tried
to clean it with his shirt. He'd like to wash
his hands, his heart. He stood all night, outside

early bird commuters, train doors shutting
a misted sun, weekday morning. Nothing

Night Shift

Nakedness troubles the nightwatchman
and day brings nakedness to everything
innocent and fertile, strips things down

the night river is a length of tarred high road
a primeval orchard on its banks nothing more
than a graveyard for old Fords

the city's full of bloodprints now
that which was merely disembodied
flips up dead

a swaying poplar on the skyline
proves to be a shock-haired demon
light corrupts

limpets shinily on surfaces
pocked and defined four heels
and all those toes, remembers

everything, made his eyes hurt
as he opened the bedroom door that morning; light
chills the nightwatchman

he pulls his frayed scarf over his eyes
as dawn blazes its terrible truths
cuts him down to size

Diamonds in the Wind

As it turned out one Guy Fawkes Night
the blaze was on the Rye
these two have climbed up One Tree Hill
to see the fireworks fly

The time was mild as autumn mist
with leaves both red and brown
says he, I know an handsome place
where we two can lie down

Says she, I love your milk white skin
also your sky blue jeans
but I am just fourteen years old
and you are still fifteen

Says he, if I am still fifteen
I work my father's stall
and all your schoolmates flirt with me
for I am six foot tall

Says she, I am so very dark
as brown as any leaf
and you are fair as cricket whites
our love will come to grief

Says he, I am my father's son
but I'm my own man too
and you are brown and beautiful
as conkers in the dew

He kissed her on her red, red lips
with kisses fierce and kind
while fireworks sailed across the sky
like diamonds in the wind

And when the Christmas break was past
and Ramadan begun
she told her best friend at the school
the deeds that they had done

And when the frost and snow was past
and leaves grew on the vine
her mother cried both day and night
saying, you're no child of mine

When the March wind turned to sun
and grapes showed on the vine
his father said, give up this girl
or you're no child of mine

And when her brother came to hear
he vowed he'd take a life
he searched the Rye and One Tree Hill
armed with a pocket knife

The boy took all his father's notes
fruit and veg as well
he made a tryst to meet his love
down in Camberwell

They rode high and they rode low
by bus and coach and train
until they reached fair Aberdeen
all in the wind and rain

And he became a marketman
with butter, eggs and cheese
saying, what is good for mum and dad
is good for you and me

Long, long may the oil rigs stand
above the breakers high
before they'll see a red red bus
come rolling past the Rye

Long, long may his father wait
by the fruit stall down East Lane
thinking of his own dear son
he never will see again

Long, long may her mother weep
as rain on Brockwell pool
before she sees her own dear girl
come giggling home from school

And long they roam the shore and mourn
for those they've left behind
but there are fireworks in the sky
and diamonds in the wind

The Very Very Song

♩=130

Dm   A   Gm/B♭   A⁷

The ve-ry ve-ry ve-ry fir-st time that I__ saw my

Dm   Dm   A

love, He was walk-ing by the ve-ry sea__ side and his

Gm/B♭   A⁷   Dm   F

ey-es were like doves. Oh__ why are__ you__

C   Dm   A

walk-ing when I'm sure you__ could__ fly, I

Dm   A

ne-ver ne-ver would have seen__ you if

Gm/B♭   A⁷   Dm

I had flown too high.

The Very Very Song

The very very very first time that I saw my love
He was walking by the very seaside & his eyes were like doves
Oh why are you walking when I'm sure you could fly
I never never would have seen you if I had flown too high

The very very very first time my love and I did stand
The sound of his very voice was like rain on parched ground
Oh why are you talking when I'm sure you could sing
Singing is for blackbirds and you're the one for me

The very very very first time my love and I sat down
The touch of his hand made my very heart grow fond
Oh why are we talking when I'm sure we could kiss
You're very very very fast girl and I like you for this

The very very very first time my love and I did kiss
The taste of his lips was like honey in a dish
Oh why only one kiss when I'm sure we could have ten
You're very very very bold girl and I'll kiss you again

The very very very first night my love and I were wed
We laid ourselves down on a very double bed
Oh why only one sheet when I know we've got more
I'm very very very sure girl that I can keep you warm

The very very very storms in the ocean find rest
When I and my true love lie snug in one nest
The very very very small birds glide over the sky
The very very wide world's in my very true love's eye

War Widow

An unexciting man, warm and quiet
in bed, safe, he dreamed he'd lost his breath
at ninety-one, it was a perfect death

Wednesday, dear, she'd squeezed his arm, *your turn*,
He's shamming sleep, she told herself, *I'll make it*,
an unobliging man, though warm and quiet

On her feet now, wandering to the kitchen
she thought, One day he won't wake up, oh yes
at ninety-one, it'd be a perfect death

She leaned inside the oven door, confused
shuffled back and jogged him, *There's no milk pet*,
an unresponsive man, warm and quiet

He looked her in the eye and seemed to grin,
Jack, it's Wednesday… Jack… run out of breath
at ninety-one, it is a perfect death

First time she's cried for sixty years – the day
that telegram… some things you don't forget…
This unexciting man, warm and quiet
at ninety-one has had the perfect death

A Measure of Expropriation

He sprints across the back; no lights; a chill of fear;
rams the metal in the wood, yanks it, bolts the front door
breathes out and cops a look around: not much to eat
grabs an apple from a bowl, helps himself to chocolate
glancing out the window, makes some calls – long distance
shaking a bit, puts on a shirt, some Mozart, stands and listens
finds a fiver in a pot, goes for a piss
drops his jeans, ragged on the carpet, can't resist
the way they concertina on the pile, as if
the wearer melted down – something for them (the hems are stiff
with mud) a piece of art; he's no use for a suit
selects a sweater, chinos – thick, lined jacket, goes for the boots,
picks some CDs, Ella, Clapton... hears the click
...a car door... moves... quick, out the back door... a racing bike
(he'd clocked it) tucks the chinos in, sweating – there
the broken fence... no lights, freewheels away, wind in his hair

Didn't find the gin, the bastard! he pours one, calling
the cops. His hands flex ...*she didn't set it ...mess ...appalling
...they're filth ...Rolex, laptop, cameras and the rest...*
She hates the way he lies spontaneously like that, his first
instinct, something slick... *Insured, oh yeah*, his thumb
punches the phone... something slick and cold. She stares past him:
the knackered denims – insult? gift? explanation?
– and gets herself a scotch. A Little Night Music plays on

In Lordship Lane

I go into the post office
to pay the road tax
and the TV licence
a recorded voice says
Cashier number two please
cashier number two please
we shuffle forward,
the woman with the pushchair
a man with ancient grey skin
holding his pension book
and three letters,
and me
On the safe behind the counter it says
this machine is time-locked
mind fingers, mind
fingers… *Cashier number three please*
we shuffle forward

The beggar outside Somerfields is red
in the face – cold? drink? embarrassment?
Spare a bit of change, please
spare a bit of change, please
sometimes I throw him fifty pence
today I quicken my pace
but take an anti-war leaflet
from a woman standing in the entrance
and shove it in my pocket

at the cash point a notice says
beware of thieves,
never disclose your number
to anyone
a man I've never seen before comes up, says

My friend died
two years ago
they're still lying on the beach
full sun. Fools
I've got a gammy leg
You're a nice lady
and limps away

I wait for the bus
opposite the Apollo video shop
they've cut the price of Star Wars Two
yours for only seven ninety-nine
the offer of a lifetime

The beggar's black and white dog
stares at us curiously
the beggar himself
has fallen asleep

Big houses up on the hill, smoke
rising from the east…

is this it –
after all this time
all the arguing
the voting
– all there is?

Properties of Substance

On the hills above the Crystal Palace
the decorous follies of Victorians
       (cared for once by servants
       who feather brushed their egg and arrow cornices
       scrubbed the flowering tiles below rich marble mantels
       polished up with chamois
       the shining ruby panes
       of panelled doors, leading
       past anaglypta dados
       massaged lovingly
       the handsome newel post
       ran a duster round
       a hundred curling spindles
       and shook the beds
       in every draughty
       heavy-curtained room;
       who drudged and dreamed, while Ma'am took tea
       and sometimes laudanum
       where gillyflower and hollyhock
       medlar, persimmon and pear stretched on the wall)

have now turned into squats:
      ethereal scarves
      of candle smoke
      jasmine oil and joss
      diffuse and float
      by plaster fruit and flowers
      long composted under
      layers of gloss
      the fireback is fleecy soot;
      upstairs
      Crapper's pale blue porcelain roses
      in a crazed bowl
      are mulched and watered frequently
      behind a door without a handle;
      people settle
      onto floorboards, share a spliff or two
      thin cheroots
      home-grown where thistles bloom
      in gardened mattresses –
the houses stand   watch…

Babies in Buggies

All down my road there are babies in buggies
six on the corner, their mothers are chatting
they fill up the pavement, the babies are sleeping
or grizzling or chucking their toys in the road

All down Northcross Road there are babies in buggies
parked outside the caff where their fathers are sitting
or they're stood in the queue for the organic grocer's
and keeping in touch with their feminine side

In the Lane are two grannies with babies in buggies
anxious to cross when the green man lights up
while in Budgens two granddads with babies in buggies
are buying them comics and sweets and toy cars

All round there are people with babies in buggies
I'm not sure if they're mummies or grannies or daddies
or granddads or sisters or brothers or snatchers
or someone's long-suffering and ill-paid au pair

I love all these babies in buggies a-trundling
the pavements of Dulwich and I can't help thinking
of all of the couplings not condommed or cautious
both loving and loveless, both randy and raucous

both long-planned and random these comings-together
black and black, white and white, black and white and all shades
that led to these blond, auburn, brown, black and straight-haired
and curly and almost bald babies in buggies

and I think of their future, these babies in buggies
enough food, enough sleep, enough space, enough play
enough dreams, enough peace, enough love, enough care
enough freedom and fun to be happy and kind

all fleetfoot and friendly and literate and lively
not too fat not too thin, not too dumb not too wise
not too shy not too wild, not too tall not too short
and what if they are: they'll have friends and relations

who'll love them regardless for just being themselves,
these babies in buggies, who'll grow old, very old
feeling fitter than fiddles, and brighter than buttons
when they're just ninety-five or a hundred-and-two

with no need for false gods or mad kings or fat profits
or dictators and bloodfeuds and wars of revenge
with fresh dreams and fresh air not polluted or poisoned
there'll be wild flowers and hedges and songbirds and trees

The streets are alive with these babies in buggies
saying, 'bye-bye', and waving and wiggling their toes
I'm just off to fetch today's paper myself:
there'll be good news – and I am Marie of Romania

Bury St Edmunds

They've preserved the elegant remains
of medieval mystery
almost intact, strong gatehouses
guard the towerless cathedral
inside its gardened close
a gothic arch, newly cleaned
(paid for by trade, for heritage is costly)
restrains a cobbled thoroughfare.
The fast food outlets also
filter their fetching scents
through old stone walls, traffic
grumbles in a circle outside
the castellated masonry, now
pale as honeycomb

It's a Friday, seven-thirty,
the taverns, open since the morning
offer up ripe jokes and local ale
somebody pisses in the street, honouring
the memory of every villein
who watered so on fair and holy days
another staggers to a lamp post
(self-conscious reproduction Deco)
Fuck off, he shouts, *fuck off!*
The autumn Suffolk air is dull and close

Friday night. The city sighs its half-fledged lechers
from the pubs, they blink, fall into step
feel the power, maraud
about the almost stylish malls;
electric country music rives the sleep of elders
and night turns rancorous

Fuckoff! They shout, *fuckoff!* There is release
tradition and communion in the effing
arrows thwacked home from taut bows –
f'ckoff!! A Christian bell ding-dongs in synchrony –
fu-ckoff. They chorus by the Shire Hall
peal past the trendier bars
the little theatre where the local rep
plays Chaucer, funded by Eastern Arts

Lords of Misrule swagger in the Burger King
mouthily demand a Whopper
leer and sway and sing
on this their own and ancient payday

In the Balti House

How come we were there in that dim Camden café
eating bhindi and naan bread, at half way to midnight
John Rety and Susan and me

when these four men burst in with a noise like a shotgun
shouting, Who loves you baby! and waking the dead
John starts up, alarmed, Let's get out

but the four settle down to a meal and a quarrel
just us and them and the white shrouded tables
the waiter on edge at the bar

Where did she come from, the girl in the black coat,
why didn't we see her, so pale and intense
till she gestured and started to speak?

I'm sat here between you, these four cursing drunkards
and you talking poetry, quite a big chasm
my father's a poet, he's good

he once read hereabouts, Torriano, the place was,
They run it, I say, John Rety and Susan,
John puts his head down and waits

He'd just started to read when a fellow walked in
with a dog, a big dog and it wouldn't stop barking
just ten years ago, she speaks on,

there was quite a kerfuffle, I'll never forget it
some shouted, Be off, and some cried, Let him stay
My boyfriend threw dog and man out.

He was never the same, my friend with the dog
after that, John looks up, he's dead, by the way,
in a fire, some said suicide

I've always felt guilty, I should have done something
led him out gently, or calmed down the dog
they didn't mean anyone harm.

How come we're alone in this dark little place
at a quarter past midnight? The clowns have gone home
and where is that girl? She's slipped out

Are they scripted, these scenes when the past histrionic
sharpshoots at the present, what actor says, *Sir,
a nice bit of Banquo along with*

your balti? Not the usual menu, an extra
then steaming white flannels to cover our faces,
the reckoning and three After Eights

Loving the Lido

We're doing our best to save it
from people who say *development*
unviable and *forward-planning*
too often,
who find it possible
to stand quite near the edge
with their clipboards and gray suits
their feet covered in shoes, their skin
never touching the water
of our Lido

We're doing our best to save it
from dull councillors and smart business persons
consortiums and quangos
hot indoor baths, jacuzzis and saunas
fitness centres with buttock-reducing contraptions
and television screens
(in case you get bored on the running machines)
where, iPod in place, you try
to work out what those moving pictures mean.

> Here, the water gives and takes light
> wind ripples it
> swimmers rearrange it in arcs and arrowheads
> their heads dipping and turning, their hands
> scattering diamonds back, oh
> the glide and splash, the dive and flash of them
> in our lido sixty-seven years beautiful. Ivies
> have scaled its LCC brick walls, trees
> grown old and tall outside, inside: a mirage
> a trompe l'oeil, an urban miracle

this oblong isle
this shining pool, always
warmer, bluer than the sky, set
in its emerald sea, reminding us
who we are, how we were

We're doing our best to save it
from *cost-benefit analysts*
public-private partnerships, regulators
inspectors and architects, their hard hats
on hard heads,
supervising wrecking balls, bulldozers
diggers and cranes progressing
their multi-level shopping mall and car park, plus
underground plunge facility
but who have made no plans for
the pair of mallard ducks
flying over from the park every evening
to join other late swimmers
in our lido

We're doing our best to save it
for the heavily pregnant young woman
now breast-stroking up and down the centre of the pool, while
her soon-to-be-born son sails under the water
in his womb-boat
backbone to the deep
dreaming now, not kicking his heels, oh
the rock and flow of it, the to and fro of it, so
this is what it's going to be like
he feels…

We're doing our best to save it
for you, little one
but so few of us are left

Dark Old Storm Cloud

Dark Old Storm Cloud

Dark old storm cloud drifted over town
Night crept in and stole the afternoon
Coldness in your eyes seems like a sign
Summer's gone... too soon

Every leaf in Regent's Park turned brown
Caught the tube and went back to your room
You talk so much I just can't read your mind
Summer's gone... too soon

    Thought I saw a smile migrating
    Across your mouth
    Must have been the last bird leaving
    On its way down south

I gaze into your face you start to frown
Sit there staring at your coffee spoon
The sun drops down behind the Northern Line
Summer's gone... too soon
Summer's gone... too soon

Stones

My city garden's full of stones brought home
in bags from beaches, black and grey and speckled
and one pale river stone from the Cevennes
smooth, cool in the hand. I've planted them

in oblong troughs, they never spread or stray
the perfect thing for lazy gardeners, neither
bolt nor wilt. Stones need no pesticide
though they may not live, they never die

What's in a stone? Sometimes calcific quirks
of beasts that couldn't carry on the race
the inside of a stone is always dark
mystery, unlived time, the universe

Slings and arrows, spark and fire, walls
– history has always needed stones
we chipped our flinty path from little piles
to cottages to monuments to malls

from bison herds to sacrificial bride
not only big Goliath that was felled
by stones; but these new days of shock and awe
they mostly represent the losing side

Plants and people multiply, bombard and
conquer; it isn't natural for stones
to fly, they're peasant missiles long outdated
but beautiful in rain, in city gardens

Gulf

Silence, empty as no man's dream
I'm a pink body hanging
suspended in my baby colour
am I born? Oh mother, let me be borne
on my cord, in this sapphire vacancy

blue. I'm tilting, turning, falling
in touchless, fruitless, birdless
say nothing, know nothing, be nothing-
ness of blue, mother of all blue

★

Arab carpet dyed in shades of earth
floats up, flattens to a threadbare, faded brown
embossed with dunes, tracks, stones
blueness retreats, holes up in the sky

★

The distant hills are green
it is a perfect day on the plain
someone is playing a pipe
there are tents, no, tabernacles
bells, long-legged shaggy goats
biblical, strolling with their keepers

A cloud of dust is moving towards me, gunfire
verily, even here. Trucks mirage from nowhere
the ground shakes, rough, ordering tongues...
one fighter down, alone, this is
the mother of all reality

Nuweiba

Go to Sharm, they said
at the kibbutz
Sharm el Sheikh, where the desert
wets the tip of its dry tongue
in the open jaws of the Red Sea
that deep water which snakes
along these coasts of Araby,
there are iridescent fish
and sharks. Mahomet's caravan
still passes, praising Allah
making his pitch.
Over on Mount Sinai,
Moses and Yahweh, ages ago
playing at thou shalt not
stitched up our morals for us

Heaving our bags on our backs
we hitched, you and me,
from Ashkelon across
the parched, cracked Negev
got stuck in Eilat
consumed fresh figs
caught a dusty truck
and came to Nuweiba
Nuweiba on the gulf of Aqaba
where the bottom jaw
pouts its lip
to Jordan and Jerusalem

oasis of the Bedouin: they stand
and amble with their camels
selling trinkets
rugs and blankets, where they sleep
nobody knows

the rest of us have stretched sarongs
between the palms
we sit beside the shack café
drinking orange juice and beer
singing Leonard Cohen songs…
Suzanne takes you down…
getting stoned
tuneless, intense, monotonous, it seems
like plainchant, merges
with the shushing sea
the heat, rocks us back
makes us remember and forget

we take off our clothes
walk among the dunes
and in a curve of sand make love
juices run, our sweat
trickles down
sand sticks to us
our backs, our thighs
to every swell and hollow
of our shared skin
if people notice us they don't stare
and if they did, neither they
nor we would care

we wash our bodies
in the blue-green Red Sea
sun dries us salty and brown
at the shack the song
is carrying on…
And the sun pours down like honey…
our lovemaking a couple of guitars
improvising
between the endless verses
of a lazy pagan psalm

suddenly the light slips away
behind the desert's tongue
into the upper jaw, the Gulf of Suez
over to the west
one gulp and everything is gone

until a hard white moon
stands up, photographs it for us
in black and white
the sea, the dunes, the palms,
shadowy, defined and still

—

Last year, someone
set off a bomb in Nuweiba
someone else
had shot some kids in Gaza
someone else
had blown up a café in Haifa
someone else
had bulldozed a whole street
and this year
someone else…

—

We never got to Sharm
infested these days with the busy rich
their summits, smiling white teeth
their flagrant
assuming charm

Nuweiba, though hardly famous
now has its Hilton too
restaurants
car parks
everything
that makes a bomb feel wanted

—

The god of love
who lay with me
in the sand, tries
to take pleasure in the garden
of his bungalow
he has trouble
with his prostate
has become
a bit of a cynic
put on weight, developed
a nervous giggle
the past
makes him turn pink

Me, I keep the guitars
the sticky sand, the moonshot
by me, in spite of the distance
between us, talisman
to cuddle up to
these empty, slippery days

Osama bin Laden

Osama bin Laden's at the bottom of my garden
I don't like to simply stand and stare
Cross-legged underneath a tree
Smiling quite outrageously
Can't think how he possibly got there
Bin Laden's in my garden, just off Cadogan Square

Osama bin Laden's not the kind to beg your pardon
Not the kind to own up to his deeds
Should I invite him to confess
Or should I phone the SAS
Should I take him down a cup of tea
Bin Laden's in my garden in SW3

Osama bin Laden is a terrorist and hard man
He's got a big black beard down to his knee
Islam's fundamental fringe
Six feet from my wheelie bins
Should I run or ring the BBC
Bin Laden's in my garden, not awfully far from me

Osama bin Laden is a fiend I could enlarge on
A rabid persecutor of the West
More evil far than Genghis Khan

Sat there on my new mown lawn
Should I place him under citizen's arrest
Bin Laden's in my garden and I'm trying to think what's best

Osama bin Laden to use departmental jargon
Was 'one of ours' in nineteen eighty four
The scourge of Soviet conscript lads
Camped beside my lily pads
Bin Laden is non grata now for sure
Bin Laden's in my garden, oh what a lovely war!

Osama bin Laden sent me hashish in a carton
In the diplomatic bag, marked for a friend
And now he wants the favour back
He thinks I'll hide him, that's a fact
But I've got truth and freedom to defend
Bin Laden's in my garden and he must be round the bend

Osama bin Laden's at the bottom of my garden
'Cos I was once his minder, don't you know
I'll take this pistol from my drawer
And fit the silencer before
I aim it where my rambling roses grow
Bin Laden's in my garden and it's time for him to go
Bin Laden's in my garden, I'm afraid he's got to go

Hearing Eye Publications in 2004–06

FROM COOKIE TO WITCH Leah Fritz
With woodcuts by Emily Johns:
£9   ISBN: 1 870841 97 2

FRIENDS IN THE COUNTRY Sarah Lawson
£3   ISBN: 1 870841 08 5

NAMASTE: NEPAL POEMS William Oxley
£6.50   ISBN: 1 870841 95 6

PODDING PEAS Valeria Melchioretto
£3   ISBN: 1 870841 54 9

PRAGUE WINTER Gerda Mayer
£8.95   ISBN: 1 870841 12 3

BLACK FLAME Sara Boyes
£3   ISBN: 1 870841 25 5

ODD BEHAVIOUR Paul Birtill
£3   ISBN: 1 870841 51 4

ACCESS BOLD AS LOVE Ray Willmott
£3   ISBN: 1 870841 47 6

THE SORCERER'S ARC June English
£6.95   ISBN: 1 870841 09 3

THE USHER'S TORCH Linda Rose Parkes
£6.95   ISBN: 1 870841 98 0

SONGS FROM THE FLATS Anna Robinson
£3   ISBN: 1 905082 01 0

SARDINIA WITHOUT LAWRENCE Nigel Foxell
£7.95   ISBN: 1 870841 86 7

WIDE SKIES, SALT AND BEST BITTER Peter Phillips
£6.95   ISBN: 1 905082 03 7

GOING ON Pat Arrowsmith
£3.00   ISBN: 1 905082 02 9

HOME, BLOODY HOME Miroslav Jancic
£9.99   ISBN: 1 905082 05 3

MIXED CONCRETE Johannes Kerkhoven
£9.99   ISBN: 1 905082 06 1

THE CEDAR FOREST Jane Elder
£9   ISBN: 1 905082 00 2

BROWN LINOLEUM GREEN LAWNS
Peter Campbell
£6.00   ISBN: 1 905082 04 5

For information about forthcoming publications, or our catalogue of books (1987-2003), please send an SSAE. All orders are attended to by return of post. You may also like to see our new website where you can order all our books online.

**Hearing Eye, Box 1,
99 Torriano Avenue,
London, NW5 2RX
www.hearingeye.org
Tel: 0207 267 2751
books@hearingeye.org**

Paper-cut by Emily Johns

We are grateful for assistance from Arts Council England, London.